Supermarket Language

A SURVIVAL VOCABULARY

Jim Richey
Reading Specialist

Illustrated by Martin Salvador

GLOBE FEARON EDUCATIONAL PUBLISHER
A Division of Simon & Schuster
Upper Saddle River, New Jersey

Janus Survival Vocabulary Books
Banking Language
Clothing Language
Credit Language
Driver's License Language
Drugstore Language
Entertainment Language
Job Application Language
Medical Language
Restaurant Language
Supermarket Language

Printed in the United States of America
  2 3 4 5 6 7 8 9 10   99 98

ISBN 0-8359-1510-7

GLOBE FEARON EDUCATIONAL PUBLISHER
A Division of Simon & Schuster
Upper Saddle River, New Jersey

Contents

Introduction

Have you ever gone shopping in a supermarket? Big place, isn't it?

Lots of things to buy.

Lots of signs.

Lots of words.

If you can read the signs and the words, you've got it made. You can find most of the things you want without too much trouble.

If you can't read all the signs and words, you've got a problem. You have to ask where everything is, go around looking for things you know by sight, or bring someone along to help you.

This book can help you shop on your own in a supermarket. It will help you learn most of the words you need to know — and a few other things besides.

Unit One

Aisle (IGHL). The walkways between the shelves (SHELVZ) are called aisles. Each aisle has a number. Each side may have a letter.

What is the number of the aisle shown above? _____ What side is the coffee on? _____ What side is the soap on? _____

Pretest

- ☐ wax
- ☐ soap
- ☐ softener
- ☐ bleach
- ☐ starch

- ☐ fish
- ☐ ham
- ☐ beef
- ☐ chicken
- ☐ turkey

- ☐ tea
- ☐ coffee
- ☐ juice
- ☐ cereal
- ☐ eggs

Words in Sentences

Circle the supermarket word in the sentence.

Soap (SOHP) Let's buy a bar of hand (soap.)
Wax (WAKS) Use wax to make the floor shine.
Bleach (BLEECH) A little bleach can make white clothes whiter.
Starch (STAHRCH) He likes to starch his shirt so it doesn't wrinkle easily.
Softener (SAWF uh ner) Put softener in the washer or dryer to make your clothes fluffy.

Same Words

Check the word at the right that is the same as the one at the left. Go as fast as you can. Time yourself. The first one is done for you.

Soap	Soup	Soap ✓	Starch	Spice
Softener	Often	Softer	Softly	Softener
Wax	Ways	Wax	Was	Tax
Starch	Starch	Start	March	Steaks
Bleach	Bread	Reach	Black	Bleach

No. Correct _____
Time _____

Pick a Word

Underline the word that belongs in the space. Then write the word in the space. The first is done for you.

Make your clothes fluffy with ____**softener**____.
bleach   soap   <u>softener</u>

Shine the floor with _____.
cheese   beer   wax

_____ makes things white.
Wax   Tea   Bleach

Wash your hands with _____.
soup   soap   starch

_____ makes things stiff.
Bleach   Soap   Starch

He likes to starch his shirt so it doesn't wrinkle easily.

*You will see respellings like this after each new word in this book. To learn how to use the respellings, see page 48.

Missing Words

Fill in the missing words. The words all come from the list on page 6. Try to write the words without looking back. The first one is done for you.

Shine the floor with _____ **wax** _____ .

Wash your hands with _____ .

_____ makes things white.

_____ makes things stiff.

Make clothes fluffy with _____ .

Scrambled Letters

The letters in each of the words are mixed up. Write the letters so they spell the words from the list on page 6. The first one is done for you.

poas _____ **soap** _____

nerefsot _____

charts _____

calheb _____ .

xaw _____ .

Missing Vowels

To find the words, fill in the missing vowels (a, e, i, o, u). Write the complete words on the blank lines. The first one is done for you.

wx _____ **wax** _____

strch _____

sftnr _____

sp _____

blch _____ .

This supermarket has fresh fish.

Words in Sentences

Circle the supermarket word in the sentence.

Fish (FISH) This supermarket has fresh fish.

Ham (HAM) We want to buy some ham to make sandwiches.

Chicken (CHIK uhn) I prefer white chicken meat, but sometimes it is dry.

Beef (BEEF) Beef is high in fat content and cholesterol.

Turkey (TER kee) My mother always cooks a turkey for the holiday dinner.

Same Words

Check the word at the right that is the same as the one at the left. Go as fast as you can. Time yourself.

Ham	Ram	Lamb	Hand	Ham
Chicken	Checkers	Chicken	Chosen	Frozen
Fish	Dish	Fresh	Fish	Wish
Turkey	Turkey	Trucker	Turning	Trouble
Beef	Beet	Berry	Beef	Reef

No. Correct _____

Time _____

Pick a Word

Underline the word that belongs in the space. Then write the word in the space.

A _____ lays eggs.

ham   chicken   starch

Steak is a kind of _____ .

fish   chicken   beef

_____ comes from a pig.

Ham   Lamb   Beef

A _____ is a big bird.

steak   bleach   turkey

We get _____ from the sea.

chicken   fish   turkey

9

Missing Words

Fill in the missing words. The words all come from the list on page 6. Try to write the words without looking back.

_____ comes from a pig.

We get _____ from the sea.

A _____ is bigger than a chicken.

A _____ lays eggs like a turkey does.

Steaks are a kind of _____.

Missing Ink

Complete the words below by adding a curve or a straight line to each letter. Then write the words on the blank lines. The first one is done for you.

CHICKEN _____ CHICKEN _____

BEEF _____

FISH _____

TURKEY _____

HAM _____

Word Wheel

Begin at start. Find the first word. Put a line between it and the next word. One set of words follows another. Write the words on the lines as you find them. The first is done for you.

_____ HAM _____

_____

_____

_____

Start ➡ H A M/T U R K E Y B E E F C H I C K E N F I S H

Check the ingredients label on the cereal box.

Words in Sentences

Circle the supermarket word in the sentence.

Tea (TEE) I like to make tea in a teapot.
Coffee (KAW fee) Coffee is made from beans that are roasted.
Juice (JOOS) Fruit juice is very good for your health.
Cereal (SIR ee uhl) Check the ingredients label on the cereal box.
Eggs (egz) Brown and white eggs taste the same.

Same Words

Check the word at the right that is the same as the one at the left. Go as fast as you can. Time yourself.

Coffee	Cookie	Coffee	Cakes	Crackers
Tea	Tee	Tree	Sea	Tea
Eggs	Edge	Eggs	Legs	Begs
Cereal	Cereal	Serious	Create	Syrup
Juice	Jump	Jam	Juice	Jelly

No. Correct _____
Time _____

Pick a Word

Underline the word that belongs in the space. Then write the word in the space.

Eat _____ with milk.
    bleach   soap   cereal

Many people like iced _____ .
    break   tea   eggs

Do you like hot _____ in the morning?
    coffee   cheese   cream

I like orange _____ in the morning.
    juice   steaks   coffee

Ham goes with _____ .
    wax   eggs   starch

11

Missing Words

Fill in the missing words. The words all come from the list on page 6. Try to write the words without looking back.

Many people like iced _____ .

I like orange _____ in the morning.

Ham goes with _____ .

Do you like hot _____ in the morning?

Eat _____ with milk.

Scrambled Letters

The letters in each of the words are mixed up. Write the letters so they spell words from the list on page 6.

gesg _____ .

eat _____ .

reclea _____ .

cuije _____ .

foecef _____ .

Missing Vowels

To find the words, fill in the missing vowels. Write the complete words on the blank lines.

crl _____ .

ta _____ .

ggs _____ .

jce _____ .

cffe _____ .

Unit One
Review

The 15 words listed below are hidden in the puzzle. They are all printed in a straight line. But they may read across, up, down, backwards or on a slant. Circle the words and phrases as you find them. Then cross them off the list. One word is done for you.

~~WAX~~	BEEF
SOAP	CHICKEN
SOFTENER	TURKEY
BLEACH	TEA
STARCH	EGGS
FISH	COFFEE
HAM	CEREAL
JUICE	

```
T A E T U R K E Y B J B
E N E K C I H C I U J E
A X X A E P J U I L I E
Y R A M R O K C G G E F
S T W Z A R E E G G S I
C O F F E E A L B I E S
C H M M O H S T A R C H
A A K L C L A E R E C C
H T S A X H B O L O K H
W C E M S O F T E N E R
P L B N O I J A N U S A
B R S C D F F N P A O S
```

Test

Complete the sentences. Write the letter of the word that fits best on the blank line. One is done for you.

Part A

1. Softeners _____ C _____. A. swim
2. Fish _____. B. soap
3. Drink _____. C. soften
4. Wash with _____. D. beef
5. Eat _____. E. tea

Part B

1. Wax _____ . A. juice
2. Drink _____ . B. shines
3. Chickens lay _____ . C. bird
4. Eat eggs and _____ . D. ham
5. A turkey is a big _____ . E. eggs

Part C

1. Bleach makes clothes __ . A. morning
2. Starch makes clothes ___ . B. stiff
3. An egg comes from a __ . C. coffee
4. Eat cereal in the _____ . D. white
5. Many people drink ____ . E. chicken

13

Unit Two

Sorry about that.

Manager (MAN ij er) If you have a problem, see the manager. The manager is the boss of the store.

When might you want his or her help? _____

_____

_____

Pretest

- ☐ bread
- ☐ crackers
- ☐ muffins
- ☐ pasta
- ☐ rice
- ☐ cakes
- ☐ cookies
- ☐ ice cream
- ☐ pies
- ☐ pastries
- ☐ nuts
- ☐ gum
- ☐ chips
- ☐ candy
- ☐ raisins

Words in Sentences

Circle the supermarket word in the sentence.

Bread (BRED) Do you like white bread or whole wheat?

Crackers (KRAK erz) These new crackers are made with no fat or salt.

Muffins (MUHF uhns) You can buy muffins, or you can buy a box of muffin mix.

Pasta (PAH stuh) Pasta is easy to make, and it gives you a lot of energy.

Rice (REYES) She makes a delicious dish with chicken and rice.

Same Words

Check the word at the right that is the same as the one at the left. Go as fast as you can. Time yourself.

Pasta	Paste	Pasta	Patsy
Muffins	Muffler	Cookies	Muffins
Crackers	Cookies	Crackers	Cakes
Bread	Break	Brad	Bread
Rice	Rice	Reed	Race

No. Correct _____

Time _____

Pick a Word

Underline the word that belongs in the space. Then write the word in the space.

_____ look like cupcakes.

Muffins	Crackers	Chips

We like to eat _____ with beans.

muffins	wax	rice

_____ comes in many shapes.

Rice	Coffee	Pasta

Did you buy a loaf of _____ ?

flour	bread	macaroni

_____ are often salty.

Crackers	Muffins	Cookies

Pasta is easy to make, and it gives you a lot of energy.

15

Missing Words

Fill in the missing words. The words all come from the list on page 14. Try to write the words without looking back.

_____ are often salty.

_____ look like cupcakes.

We like to eat _____ with beans.

_____ comes in many shapes.

Did you buy a loaf of _____?

Missing Ink

Complete the words below by adding a curve or a straight line to each letter. Then write the words on the blank lines.

MUFFINS _____

CRACKERS _____

PASTA _____

RICE _____

BREAD _____

Word Wheel

Begin at start. Find the first word. Put a line between it and the next word. One set of words follows another. Write the words on the lines as you find them.

_____

_____

_____

_____

Start ➡ B R E A D P A S T A R I C E C R A C K E R S M U F F I N S

Words in Sentences

Circle the supermarket word in the sentence.

Cakes (KAYKS) This supermarket makes birthday cakes.

Cookies (KUK eez) Their favorite cookies are chocolate chip.

Ice Cream (IGHS KREEM) I always eat chocolate cake with ice cream for my birthday.

Pastries (PAYS treez) You must keep these pastries in the refrigerator.

Pies (PIGHZ) I like cherry and apple pies.

Same Words

Check the word at the right that is the same as the one at the left. Go as fast as you can. Time yourself.

Pastries	Paste	Pastries	Paris
Ice Cream	Ice Milk	Ice Cream	Nice Dream
Cakes	Bakes	Cakes	Cookies
Pies	Piles	Ties	Pies
Cookies	Rookies	Cakes	Cookies

No. Correct _____

Time _____

Pick a Word

Underline the word that belongs in the space. Then write the word in the space.

_____ is always cold.

Pie   Pudding   Ice Cream

Some people like a few _____ with coffee.

brooms   cookies   turkeys

_____ have a crust.

Pies   Cakes   Ice Cream

Did you ever get two birthday _____ ?

eggs   cakes   crackers

_____ come in many shapes and flavors.

Pastries   Ice Cream   Shoes

This supermarket makes birthday cakes.

17

Missing Words

Fill in the missing words. The words all come from the list on page 14. Try to write the words without looking back.

_____ have a crust.

Some people like a few _____ with coffee.

_____ is always cold.

_____ come in many shapes and flavors.

Did you ever get two birthday _____?

Scrambled Letters

The letters in each of the words are mixed up. Write the letters so they spell words from the list on page 14.

skieoco _____

spei _____

cie marce _____

sckea _____

spstraei _____

Missing Vowels

To find the words, fill in the missing vowels. Write the complete words on the blank lines.

ce crm _____

ps _____

cks _____

pstrs _____

coks _____

Words in Sentences

Circle the supermarket word in the sentence.

Gum (GUHM) This gum has too much sugar in it.

Chips (CHIPS) We buy corn chips to eat with salsa and cheese.

Candy (KAN dee) After dinner, he always eats a small piece of chocolate candy.

Raisins (RAYZ uhns) She eats cereal with raisins and milk for breakfast.

Nuts (NUHTS) Some candy has nuts and raisins.

We buy corn chips to eat with salsa and cheese.

Same Words

Check the word at the right that is the same as the one at the left. Go as fast as you can. Time yourself.

Candy	Candy	Corny	Sandy	Dandy
Chips	Chops	Hips	Chips	Chirps
Gum	Gun	Gum	Glum	Grin
Raisins	Poisons	Risen	Raising	Raisins
Nuts	Not	Ruts	Nuts	Guts

No. Correct _____

Time _____

Pick a Word

Underline the word that belongs in the space. Then write the word in the space.

_____ are dried grapes.

　　Raisins　　　　　Nuts　　　　　Prunes

Do you chew _____ ?

　　gun　　　　　flour　　　　　gum

Did you buy a _____ bar?

　　ham　　　　　candy　　　　　Macaroni

_____ go with dips.

　　Pies　　　　　Chips　　　　　Gums

_____ come with or without a shell.

　　Raisins　　　　　Cakes　　　　　Nuts

Missing Words

Fill in the missing words. The words all come from the list on page 14. Try to write the words without looking back.

_____ go with dips.

_____ come with or without a shell.

_____ are dried grapes.

Did you buy a _____ bar?

Do you chew _____ ?

Missing Ink

Complete the words below by adding a curve or a straight line to each letter. Then write the words on the blank lines.

RAISINS _____

CANDY _____

CHIPS _____

GUM _____

NUTS _____

Word Wheel

Begin at start. Find the first word. Put a line between it and the next word. One set of words follows another. Write the words on the lines as you find them.

_____

_____

_____

_____

_____

Start ▶ R A I S I N S G U M C H I P S C A N D Y N U T S

Review

The fifteen words from Unit 2 fit into this puzzle. They go across and down. The sentences and number of spaces will help you. As you find the words, write them in the spaces in the sentences. One is done for you.

Across

3. Do you like **ice cream** cones?
5. _____ go with dips.
7. You can buy a _____ bar.
10. _____ are good in the morning.
11. _____ are dried grapes.
12. You can buy _____ in the shell.
13. Get a loaf of _____.
14. Many people like _____ salad.

Down

1. You bake _____ in the oven.
2. Do you like chewing _____?
4. _____ are often salty.
5. Bake _____ in the oven, too.
6. _____ are sweet and have a crust.
8. _____ are fancy baked goods such as pies.
9. We like to eat beans and _____.

Test

Put a + beside each sentence that is true. Put a ○ if it is not true.

_____ 1. Pasta is another name for pastries.

_____ 2. Candy is sweet.

_____ 3. Ice cream is cold.

_____ 4. Nuts are made from raisins.

_____ 5. Muffins are pies.

_____ 6. Bread is made from flour.

_____ 7. Gum is to chew, not to eat.

_____ 8. Crackers are cereals.

_____ 9. Cakes and cookies are breads.

_____ 10. Chips go well with dips.

Unit Three

Please Return Carts Here. Most supermarkets have a special place to leave shopping carts. How does it help everyone if you put your cart there? _____
_____
_____

Pretest

- ☐ mustard
- ☐ relish
- ☐ catsup
- ☐ olives
- ☐ pickles
- ☐ spices
- ☐ dressing
- ☐ sugar
- ☐ vinegar
- ☐ salad oil
- ☐ milk
- ☐ cheese
- ☐ butter
- ☐ sour cream
- ☐ margarine

Words in Sentences

Circle the supermarket word in the sentence.

Mustard (MUHS terd) They can save money on mustard.

Relish (REL uhsh) They eat mustard and relish on hot dogs.

Catsup (KECH uhp) Many people put catsup on their eggs.

Olives (AHL ivz) He loves to eat green olives.

Pickles (PIK uhlz) These pickles taste very sour.

They can save money on mustard.

Same Words

Check the word at the right that is the same as the one at the left. Go as fast as you can. Time yourself.

Relish	Polish	Relish	Relief	Release
Olives	Lives	Older	Olives	Alive
Mustard	Custard	Master	Muster	Mustard
Catsup	Catsup	Catcher	Supper	Cater
Pickles	Picnics	Puddings	Nickels	Pickles

No. Correct _____

Time _____

Pick a Word

Underline the word that belongs in the space. Then write the word in the space.

_____ are almost always green.

Bread   Pickles   Juice

_____ can be black or green.

Olives   Coffee   Mustard

_____ is red.

Bleach   Macaroni   Catsup

_____ is yellow.

Catsup   Mustard   Pickle

_____ can be made from olives, pickles, mustard, and catsup.

Cookies   Cereal   Relish

23

Missing Words

Fill in the missing words. The words all come from the list on page 22. Try to write the words without looking back.

_____ can be black or green.

_____ is red.

_____ are almost always green.

_____ is yellow.

_____ can be made from olives, pickles, mustard, and catsup.

Scrambled Letters

The letters in each of the words are mixed up. Write the letters so they spell words from the list on page 22.

rustdam _____

lipseck _____

patcus _____

voisel _____

hersil _____

Missing Vowels

To find the words, fill in the missing vowels. Write the complete word on the blank space.

rlsh _____

ctsp _____

lvs _____

mstrd _____

pckls _____

Words in Sentences

Circle the supermarket word in the sentence.

Spices (SPIGH suhz) Spices add flavor to cookies and pies.

Sugar (SHUG er) Sugar makes desserts taste sweet.

Dressing (DRES ing) I like French dressing on my salad.

Salad Oil (SAL uhd OIL) Can I use salad oil to make muffins?

Vinegar (VIN uh ger) We can make a salad dressing from oil and vinegar.

Same Words

Check the word at the right that is the same as the one at the left. Go as fast as you can. Time yourself.

Sugar	Shorter	Slugger	Sugar
Dressing	Dressing	Blessing	Drying
Salad Oil	Soft Boil	Salad Oil	Salute
Spices	Specials	Soaps	Spices
Vinegar	Vigor	Vinegar	Winter

No. Correct ‗‗‗‗‗‗‗

Time ‗‗‗‗‗‗‗

Pick a Word

Underline the word or phrase that belongs in the space. Then write the word or phrase in the space.

‗‗‗‗‗‗‗‗‗‗‗‗‗‗‗‗‗‗ and oil make a good dressing.

Vinegar	Salad Oil	Catsup

‗‗‗‗‗‗‗‗‗‗‗‗‗‗‗‗‗‗‗‗ is put on salads.

Dressing	Baby food	Flour

Most candy has lots of ‗‗‗‗‗‗‗‗‗‗‗‗‗‗ .

diet food	sugar	steaks

Salt and pepper are ‗‗‗‗‗‗‗‗‗‗‗‗‗‗ .

sugar	raisins	spices

Can I use salad oil to make muffins?

Missing Words

Fill in the missing words. The words all come from the list on page 22. Try to write the words without looking back.

_____ can be red or white.

You put _____ on salads.

You can fry with _____ .

Salt and pepper are _____ .

Most candy has lots of _____ .

Missing Ink

Complete the words below by adding a curve or a straight line to each letter. Then write the words on the blank lines.

SALAD OIL _____

VINEGAR _____

DRESSING _____

SUGAR _____

SPICES _____

Word Wheel

Begin at Start. Find the first word or phrase. Put a line between it and the next word or phrase. One set of words follows another. Write the words on the lines as you find them.

_____

_____

_____

_____

_____

Start ➡ DRESSINGSUGARSPICESSALADOILVINEGAR .

Words in Sentences

Circle the supermarket word in the sentence.

Milk (MILK) The milk that is called 1% and 2% is low fat.

Cheese (CHEEZ) Is this cheese good for pizza?

Butter (BUHT er) A box of butter can come in four sticks.

Sour Cream (SOWR KREEM) Sour cream is very good on tacos and tostadas.

Margarine (MAHRJ uh ruhn) Margarine has less cholesterol than butter.

Same Words

Check the word at the right that is the same as the one at left. Go as fast as you can. Time yourself.

Butter	Better	Button	Butter
Cheese	Cheese	Cheat	Breeze
Margarine	Margaret	Marjaram	Margarine
Sour Cream	Sour Dream	Sour Cream	Ice Cream
Milk	Silk	Milt	Milk

No. Correct _____

Time _____

Pick a Word

Underline the word or phrase that belongs in the space. Then write the word or phrase in the space.

Many people like macaroni and _____ .

cheese   breeze   brooms

_____ is white and comes from a cow.

Silk   Milk   Margarine

_____ is yellow and put on bread.

Sour cream   Dressing   Butter

_____ looks like butter.

Catsup   Margarine   Milk

_____ is always white and is made from milk.

Sour cream   Mustard   Macaroni

Is this cheese good for pizza?

Missing Words

Fill in the missing words. The words all come from the list on page 22. Try to write the words without looking back.

_____ is white and comes from a cow.

_____ is yellow and put on bread.

Many people like macaroni and _____ .

_____ is always white and is made

from milk.

_____ looks like butter.

Scrambled Letters

The letters in each of the words are mixed up. Write the letters so they spell words from the list on page 22.

ruso merac _____

ginramare _____

scheee _____

limk _____

tubret _____

Missing Vowels

To find the words, fill in the missing vowels. Write the complete words on the blank lines.

mlk _____

bttr _____

mrgrn _____

chs _____

sr crm _____

Review

The fifteen words or phrases from the list on page 22 fit in this puzzle. The first and last letters of each word are given. The letters where the words cross are also given. Fill in the missing letters. Don't look back unless you have to. One is done for you.

```
                    ¹M                        ²V
        ³S O U R C R E A M   ⁴S   I           S
        ⁵M       A   ⁶D       ⁷R       H
                              ⁸B
                    ⁹S       R
            E                     
        ¹⁰P I     L   S   ¹¹C   T       P
            G         ¹²M
                    ¹³O   I   E S
                    L   K   E
```

Test

Complete the sentences. Write the letter of the word or phrase that fits *best* on the blank line.

Part A

1. Sour cream is _____ .   A. yellow
2. Catsup is _____ .   B. red
3. Butter is _____ .   C. sweet
4. Salt and pepper are _ .   D. white
5. Sugar is _____ .   E. spices

Part B

1. Fry with _____ .   A. milk
2. Drink _____ .   B. cheese
3. Eat _____ .   C. yellow
4. Mustard is _____ .   D. salad oil
5. Pickles are _____ .   E. green

Part C

1. Butter looks like ____ .   A. olives, pickles, mustard, and catsup
2. Olives are _____ .   B. salads
3. Relish is made from _ .   C. green or black
4. Dressing is good on ____ .   D. dressing
5. Use oil and vinegar to make _ .   E. margarine

Unit Four

Press Button for Service (SER vuhs). Some stores have a bell to ring if you want someone to help you. Often there is one at the meat case. When might you want help at the meat case? _____ _____ _____

Pretest

- ☐ pound
- ☐ packages
- ☐ fruits
- ☐ produce
- ☐ vegetables
- ☐ jam
- ☐ jelly
- ☐ honey
- ☐ preserves
- ☐ syrup
- ☐ cashier
- ☐ coupons
- ☐ flyers
- ☐ discount
- ☐ scanner

Words in Sentences

Circle the supermarket word in the sentence.

Produce (PROH doos) He works in the produce department.

Fruits (FROOTS) The fruits in this department are fresh, not in cans.

Vegetables (VEJ tuh buhlz) You can see that the vegetables are fresh and clean.

Packages (PAK uh juhz) Some fruits and vegetables come in packages.

Pound (POWND) You can buy a pound of apples for $.99.

Same Words

Check the word at the right that is the same as the one at left. Go as fast as you can. Time yourself.

Vegetables	Vehicles	Vegetables	Velvets
Produce	Product	Protect	Produce
Fruits	Foot	Fruits	Flowers
Pound	Pond	Pine	Pound
Packages	Packages	Packed	Picking

No. Correct _____

Time _____

Pick a Word

Underline the word that belongs in the space. Then write the word in the space.

Produce is often sold by the _____.

    vegetables   pound   spices

Apples and oranges are _____.

    fruits   soup   vegetables

Corn and peas are _____.

    fruits   soaps   vegetables

Fruits, vegetables, and nuts are _____.

    margarine   produce   muffins

Most food comes in attractive _____.

    pound   candy   packages

He works in the produce department.

Missing Words

Fill in the missing words. The words all come from the list on page 30. Try to write the words without looking back.

Apples and oranges are _____.
Most food comes in attractive _____.
Corn and peas are _____.
Fruits, vegetables, and nuts are _____.
Produce is often sold by the _____.

Missing Ink

Complete the words below by adding a curve or straight line to each letter. Then write the words in the blank spaces.

PRODUCE _____
POUND _____
PACKAGES _____
VEGETABLES _____
FRUITS _____

Word Wheel

Begin at Start. Find the first word. Put a line between it and the next word. One word follows another. Write the words on the lines as you find them.

_____
_____
_____
_____

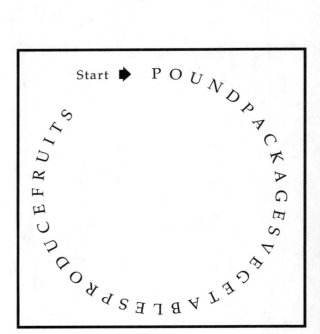

Words in Sentences

Circle the supermarket word in the sentence.

Jam (JAM) Jam can be made from many fruits.

Jelly (JEL ee) The little girl likes apple jelly.

Preserves (pri ZERVZ) Preserves are another name for jams and jellies.

Honey (HUHN ee) Honey is made by bees.

Syrup (SIR uhp) Maple syrup is made from the sap of maple trees.

Same Words

Check the word at the right that is the same as the one at left. Go as fast as you can. Time yourself.

Syrup	Stirrup	Syrup	Cycle	Soup
Jelly	Jerky	Juice	Jelly	Belly
Honey	Honey	Homey	Honest	Honor
Jam	Jar	Gum	Jaw	Jam
Preserves	Reserves	Preserves	Conserves	Prevent

No. Correct _____

Time _____

Pick a Word

Underline the word that belongs in the space. Then write the word in the space.

Bees make _____ .

    gum   honey   produce

Put _____ on pancakes.

    relish   mustard   syrup

_____ is made from fruit and sugar.

    Jelly   Catsup   Raisins

_____ is thicker than jelly.

    Juice   Jam   Tea

Jam and jelly are kinds of _____ .

    sauces   muffins   preserves

The little girl likes apple jelly.

Missing Words

Fill in the missing words. The words all come from the list on page 30. Try to write the words without looking back.

Jam and jelly are kinds of _____ .

Bees make _____ .

_____ is thicker than jelly.

Put _____ on pancakes.

_____ is made from fruit and sugar.

Scrambled Letters

The letters in each of the words are mixed up. Write the letters so they spell words from the list on page 30.

rysup _____

lyelj _____

mja _____

vesreserp _____

nohey _____

Missing Vowels

To find the words, fill in the missing vowels. Write the complete words on the blank lines.

hny _____

prsrvs _____

jm _____

srp _____

jll _____

Words in Sentences

Circle the supermarket word in the sentence.

Cashier (ka SHEER) She has a job as a supermarket cashier.

Coupons (KOO ponz) We cut coupons from the paper.

Flyers (FLIGH erz) These supermarket flyers came in the mail.

Discount (DIS kownt) Some flyers have coupons that offer discount prices.

Scanner (SKAN er) The scanner reads the bar code on the packages of food.

Same Words

Check the word at right that is the same as the word at left. Go as fast as you can. Time yourself.

Scanner	Scene	Scan	Scanner
Flyers	Flyers	Flights	Fleas
Discount	Dismiss	Dismay	Discount
Coupons	Cups	Coupons	Counts
Cashier	Cashes	Counter	Cashier

No. Correct _____

Time _____

Pick a Word

Underline the word that belongs in the space. Then write the word in the space.

People save _____ from the paper.

     cereal   coupons   cashier

_____ tell people about special sales.

     Cashiers   Flyers   Packages

The _____ rings up the prices.

     coupons   doctor   cashier

A _____ is a lower price.

     package   discount   bar code

The _____ reads the bar code on packages.

     scanner   coupons   produce

The scanner reads the bar code on the packages of food.

Missing Words

Fill in the missing words. The words all come from the list on page 30. Try to write the words without looking back.

A _____ is a low price.

Stores send _____ to tell people about sales.

A _____ rings up the prices.

We cut _____ from the paper.

A _____ reads the bar code on packages.

Missing Ink

Complete the words below by adding a curve or a straight line to each letter. Then write the words on the blank lines.

SCANNER _____

CASHIER _____

COUPONS _____

FLYERS _____

DISCOUNT _____

Word Wheel

Begin at Start. Find the first word or phrase. Put a line between it and the next word or phrase. One set of words follows another. Write the words on the lines as you find them.

_____

_____

_____

_____

_____

Review

The fifteen words from Unit 4 fit into this puzzle. They go across and down. As you find the words, write them in the spaces in the puzzle and the sentences.

Across

3. Fruit and vegetables are _____.
4. Most food comes in _____.
6. I like to put _____ on my pancakes.
9. _____ is thicker than jelly.
11. Many people like _____ with cheese and bread.
12. Corn and peas are _____.
14. People cut _____ from the paper.

Down

1. A _____ is a lower price.
2. Bees make_____.
5. The _____ adds up the prices of your food.
6. A _____ reads bar codes.
7. Jam and jelly are kinds of _____.
8. Stores send _____ to tell about sales.
10. Apples and oranges are kinds of _____.
13. You can buy produce by the _____.

Test

Put a + beside each sentence that is true. Put a ○ if it is not true.

____ 1. Apples and corn are vegetables.
____ 2. Bees make preserves.
____ 3. The cashier adds up the food prices.
____ 4. Jam and jelly are preserves.
____ 5. Syrup is sweet.
____ 6. Peas and oranges are fruits.
____ 7. Ham and cheese are produce.
____ 8. Some soup is made from vegetables.
____ 9. Some candy is sold by the pound.
____ 10. Coupons can save you money.

Unit Five

Express Line / 9 Items or Less / No Checks Cashed. Most large markets have express (ik SPRES) lines. These are for shoppers who only want a few things. How do express lines help shoppers? _____

_____

_____

Pretest

- ☐ napkins
- ☐ plastics
- ☐ tissue
- ☐ paper plates
- ☐ aluminum foil
- ☐ mixes
- ☐ condiments
- ☐ canned goods
- ☐ frozen foods
- ☐ bakery
- ☐ polish
- ☐ paper towels
- ☐ cleansers
- ☐ detergents
- ☐ liquid detergents
- ☐ charcoal
- ☐ party supplies
- ☐ picnic supplies
- ☐ beverages
- ☐ deli

Words in Sentences

Circle the supermarket word in the sentence.

Napkins (NAP kinz) Throw away napkins with other paper trash.

Plastic (PLAS tik) You should recycle plastic bottles.

Tissue (TISH oo) Please sneeze into a tissue.

Paper Plates (PAY per PLAYTS) It saves time to use paper plates because you don't wash them.

Aluminum Foil (uh LOO muh NUHM FOIL) Wrap the fish in aluminum foil to keep it fresh.

Same Words

Check the word at the right that is the same as the one at the left. Go as fast as you can. Time yourself.

Tissue	Tissue	Issue
Paper Plates	Paper Plates	Plastic Plates
Napkins	Napping	Napkins
Plastic	Plastic	Plasters
Aluminum Foil	Aluminum Boil	Aluminum Foil

No. Correct _____

Time _____

Pick a Word

Underline the word that belongs in the space. Then write the word in the space.

Many things are made from _____ .

    plates   plastic   preserves

You can eat from _____ .

    paper plates   bleach   starch

Blow your nose with _____ .

    aluminum foil   paper plates   tissue

Use a _____ to wipe your mouth.

    napkin   foil   relish

Wrap left over food in _____ .

    tissue   preserves   aluminum foil

You should recycle plastic bottles.

Missing Words

Fill in the missing words. The words all come from the list on page 38. Try to write the words without looking back.

Use a _____ to wipe your mouth.

Blow your nose with _____ .

Put left over food in _____ .

You can eat from _____ .

Many things are made from _____ .

Scrambled Letters

The letters in each of the words are mixed up. Write the letters so they spell words from the list on page 38.

unulamim loif _____

setsiu _____

reapp eatslp _____

claspit _____

skinpan _____

Missing Vowels

To find the words, fill in the missing vowels. Write the complete words on the blank lines.

plstc _____

ppr plts _____

npkns _____

lmnm fl _____

tsse _____

The machine will tell you that the soups are with the canned goods.

Words in Sentences

Circle the supermarket word in the sentence.

Mixes (MIKS uhz) I buy packaged mixes to make cakes and cookies quickly.

Canned Goods (KAND GUHDZ) The machine will tell you that the soups are with the canned goods.

Condiments (KAHN di muhnts) Mustard, relish, catsup, and mayonnaise are condiments.

Frozen Foods (FROHZ uhn FOODZ) The frozen foods department has complete dinners.

Bakery (BAYK er ee) There is fresh bread in the bakery department.

Same Words

Check the word at right that is the same as the word at left. Go as fast as you can. Time yourself.

Mixes	Mix	Mixes
Condiments	Condiments	Conditions
Frozen Foods	Freezing Foods	Frozen Foods
Bakery	Bakery	Baking Pans
Canned Goods	Canned Goods	Canned Fruits

No. Correct _____

Time _____

Pick a Word

Underline the word that belongs in the space. Then write the word in the space.

You can make cakes and cupcakes from _____.

  pasta   mixes   sugar

_____ should be kept frozen.

  Frozen foods   Fast foods   Fabrics

Pastries and bread are in the _____ department.

  pasta   produce   bakery

Mustard, catsup, and relish are _____.

  mayonnaise   preserves   condiments

Use a can opener to open _____.

  frozen foods   produce   canned goods

41

Missing Words

Fill in the missing words. The words all come from the list on page 38. Try to write the words without looking back.

Mustard and relish are kinds of _____.

You need a can opener to open _____.

_____ should be kept frozen.

The _____ department has bread and pastries.

It is quick to make cakes and cookies from _____.

Missing Ink

Complete the words below by adding a curve or a straight line to each letter. Then write the words on the blank lines.

BAKERY _____

CANNED GOODS _____

CONDIMENTS _____

FROZEN FOODS _____

MIXES _____

Word Wheel

Begin at Start. Find the first word or phrase. Put a line between it and the next word or phrase. One follows another. Write the words on the lines as you find them.

_____

_____

_____

_____

Start ➡ MIXESCONDIMENTSCANNEDGOODSBAKERYFROZENFOODS

Polish will make the floor shine.

Words in Sentences

Circle the supermarket word in the sentence.

Polish (PAHL ish) Polish will make the floor shine.

Paper Towels (PAY per TOW uhlz) Paper towels are good for wiping windows.

Cleansers (KLEN zerz) Powdered cleansers help make sinks clean again.

Detergents (dih TER juhnts) Some detergents are liquid and some are powders.

Liquid Detergents (LIK wid dih TER juhnts) Liquid detergents are good for washing dishes.

Same Words

Check the word at the right that is the same as the one at the left. Go as fast as you can. Time yourself.

Liquid Detergents	Liquor Dinners	Liquid Detergents
Cleansers	Cleaners	Cleansers
Detergents	Detergents	Dependents
Polish	Police	Polish
Paper Towels	Bath Towels	Paper Towels

No. Correct _____

Time _____

Pick a Word

Underline the word that belongs in the space. Then write the word in the space.

Wax and _____ are alike.

    shoes   polish   soup

_____ are wet before you use them.

   Liquid detergents   Raisins   Napkins

Liquid detergents and dry _____ are used to do the wash.

   soups   liquor   detergents

_____ are used to clean walls, floors, sinks, etc.

   Cleansers   Dressings   Relishes

_____ can be used and thrown away.

   Candies   Puddings   Paper towels

Missing Words

Fill in the missing words. The words all come from the list on page 38. Try to write the words without looking back.

_____ can be used and thrown away.

Liquid detergents and dry _____ are used to do the wash.

_____ are wet before you use them.

Wax and _____ are alike.

_____ are used to clean walls, floors, sinks, etc.

Scrambled Letters

The letters in each of the words are mixed up. Write the letters so they spell words from the list on page 38.

getdertsne _____

realcnses _____

diqlui _____

shiplo _____

raepp lotsew _____

Missing Vowels

To find the words, fill in the missing vowels. Write the complete words on the blank lines.

clnsrs _____

ppr twls _____

lqd dtrgnts _____

dtrgnts _____

plsh _____

**Shop for cold cuts
at the deli counter.**

Words in Sentences

Circle the supermarket word in the sentence.

Beverages (BEV rij uhs) Did you remember to buy ice to keep the beverages cold?

Charcoal (CHAHR kohl) We need charcoal to start the fire in the grill.

Party Supplies (PAHR tee suh PLIGHZ) Does this store sell party supplies?

Picnic Supplies (PIK nik suh PLIGHZ) I bought paper plates and napkins for picnic supplies.

Deli (DEL i) Shop for cold cuts at the deli counter.

Same Words

Check the word at right that is the same as the word at left. Go as fast as you can. Time yourself.

Picnic Supplies	Party Supplies	Picnic Supplies
Beverages	Leverages	Beverages
Deli	Delicious	Deli
Charcoal	Char broil	Charcoal
Party Supplies	Party Supplies	Party Surprise

No. Correct _____

Time _____

Pick a Word

Underline the word that belongs in the space. Then write the word in the space.

Use _____ when you eat in a park.
  liquid surprise   picnic supplies   pet supplies

_____ are things to drink.
  Cereal   Liquid detergents   Beverages

You can buy meat and cheeses at the _____ counter.
  delivery   deli   dedicate

You can use _____ to cook outside.
  detergents   cleansers   charcoal

When you ask many friends over, you need

_____ .

  party supplies   turkey surprise   chips and bleach

Missing Words

Fill in the missing words. The words all come from the list on page 38. Try to write the words without looking back.

You can use _____ to cook outside.

Use _____ when you eat in a park.

_____ are things to drink.

When you ask many friends over, you need

_____ .

You can buy cheese, lunch meat, and good things to

eat at a _____ .

Missing Ink

Complete the words below by adding a curve or a straight line to each letter. Then write the words on the blank lines.

CHARCOAL _____

DELI _____

PARTY SUPPLIES _____

BEVERAGES _____

PICNIC SUPPLIES _____

Word Wheel

Begin at Start. Find the first word or phrase. Put a line between it and the next word or phrase. One follows another. Write the words on the lines as you find them.

_____

_____

_____

_____

_____

Start ➡ BEVERAGESPICNICSUPPLIESDELIPARTYSUPPLIESCHARCOAL

Unit Five
Review

The 20 things listed below are hidden in the puzzle. They are all printed in a straight line. But they may read across, up, down, backwards or on a slant. Circle the words or phrases as you find them. Then cross them off the list.

CHARCOAL
PAPER TOWELS
MIXES
FROZEN FOODS
BEVERAGES
CLEANSERS
NAPKINS
PICNIC SUPPLIES
DELI
LIQUID DETERGENTS
DETERGENTS
PARTY SUPPLIES
ALUMINUM FOIL
POLISH
CONDIMENTS
CANNED GOODS
BAKERY
PAPER PLATES
TISSUE
PLASTIC

```
S U S S R E N N I D D E R A P E R P
U A L P A P E R P L A T E S K L C Y
R T I N D E L I M Y A J R J L Z L S
C E Q O P P A R T Y S U P P L I E S
S A U O P S S T N E M I D N O C A E
S F I D D E T E R G E N T S T S N I
S K D F A D B S O N I J M L C X S L
D N D G E C J R E U S S I T A Y E P
O B E V E R A G E S H O X Y N X R P
O Q T A L S F T Z N F G E Z N S S U
F X E Y B X G F Y M F N S Y E C W S
N Z R C A C D R U E M O P T D I V C
E R G D G C E N P O L I S H G T U I
Z U E F X K I D E L S R Q R O S S N
O S N A A M C F K C H A R C O A L C
R T T B U B G J T U V W X Z D L R I
F N S L A H I S N I K P A N S P Q P
W P A P E R T O W E L S H E A T G O
```

Test

Put an **E** next to anything you can eat.
Put a **D** next to anything you can drink.
Put an **F** next to anything you can use to either cook, serve, or keep food.
Put a **C** next to anything you can use to clean with.
Some items may have more than one letter.

1 ___	Charcoal	8 ___	Picnic Supplies	15 ___	Plastic
2 ___	Paper Towels	9 ___	Deli	16 ___	Tissue
3 ___	Mixes	10 ___	Liquid Detergents	17 ___	Detergents
4 ___	Frozen Foods	11 ___	Party Supplies	18 ___	Condiments
5 ___	Beverages	12 ___	Aluminum Foil	19 ___	Canned Goods
6 ___	Cleansers	13 ___	Polish	20 ___	Paper Plates
7 ___	Napkins	14 ___	Bakery		

Guide to Phonetic Respellings*

Many of the words in this book are followed by respellings. The respellings show you how to say the words.

A respelling tells you three things about a word:

1. How many sounds, or syllables, the word has
2. Which syllable to stress
3. How to say each syllable

Look at the chart below. It shows you how to say each part of a respelling.

Now look at the word below. Then look at the respelling that follows it.

example (ig ZAM puhl)

1. How many syllables does *example* have? (3)
2. Which syllable should you stress? (ZAM)
3. How do you say each syllable? (ig) (ZAM) (puhl)

Say **example** (ig ZAM puhl) out loud. Then practice saying these respellings:

practice (PRAK tuhs) **syllable** (SIL uh buhl)
follow (FAHL oh) **phonetic** (fuh NET ik)

If you see:	Say it like the:	In:	If you see:	Say it like the:	In:
(a)	a	pat	(m)	m	me
(ah)	a	father	(n)	n	no
(air)	air	fair	(ng)	ng	sing
(aw)	aw	paw	(oh)	oa	coat
(ay)	ay	day	(oi)	oy	boy
(b)	b	bee	(oo)	oo	too
(ch)	ch	chair	(or)	or	for
(d)	d	do	(ow)	ow	how
(e)	e	send	(p)	p	pay
(ee)	ee	see	(r)	r	row
(ehr)	err	merry	(s)	s	say
(er)	er	fern	(sh)	sh	she
(ear)	ear	hear	(t)	t	too
(f)	f	far	(th)	th	thin
(g)	g	go	(*th*)	th	the
(h)	h	he	(u)	u	put
(hw)	wh	where	(uh)	u	but
(i)	i	is	(v)	v	very
(igh)	igh	high	(w)	w	way
(j)	j	joy	(y)	y	you
(k)	k	key	(z)	z	zoo
(l)	l	lay	(zh)	s	treasure

*All respellings are based on pronunciations found in *Webster's New Collegiate Dictionary*, 8th ed. (Springfield, Mass.: G. & C. Merriam Co., 1974). Pronunciations may differ in your community or your geographic region.